Praise for *Ecologia*

With passion and precision, ardor and humor, Whitmanian exuberance and Dickinsonian canniness, Sophia Anfinn Tonnessen's *Ecologia* springs up from the "wounded place" that is also "holy ground." I don't know when I've read a debut collection with such panache and such depth. Tracking the poet's transition, this book discovers tremendous vitality in its gorgeous and invigorating openness to change. Here's an entirely original contribution to the mosaic of American poetry.

Peter Campion, Poet and critic, and author of *One Summer Evening at the Falls* and *Radical as Reality: Form and Freedom in American Poetry,* among other collections

Ecologia is truly a study of the home, equally comfortable exploring the room of the body as it is exploring the room of the mind, though the speaker resides in uncomfortable liminality. This first collection of poems by Tonnessen holds a Heraclitan tension on the topic of transition. From shifts of body, to shifts of love, to shifts of work, from shifts of diction and syntax, from shifts of lyricism to the more linear, this collection culminates them eruditely and with inspiring grace.

David Tomas Martinez, Poet and author of *Hustle* and *Post Traumatic Hood Disorder*

With earnestness and urgency, *Ecologia* chronicles a transformation, a translation of energy and spirit within the force and fragility of the physical body. The poems process this energy with the momentum of the natural world — a storm surge, a dazed sparrow, *a shadow passing over long grasses.* Tonnessen does not spare us the brutality of rebirth but allows relief in detailing the humor, the eroticism, and the ordinary, delicate beauty of this life. This book reminds us of what it is to inhabit a body, to live with uncertainty, to hurt and to heal, and it resonates with the humble magic of resilience: *And the grace in falling too, as rain comes to rescue. / How many times have I been buried, and come back again?*

Carey McHugh, Poet and author of *American Gramophone*

Ecologia

Ecologia Sophia
Anfinn Tonnessen

UNBOUND EDITION PRESS

Atlanta

FIRST EDITION

Printed in the United States of America

LIBRARY OF CONGRESS RECORD

Name: Tonnessen, Sophia Anfinn, 1996— author.
Title: Ecologia / Sophia Anfinn Tonnessen.
Edition: First edition.
Published: Atlanta : Unbound Edition Press, 2021.

LCCN: 2021937085
LCCN Permalink: https://lccn.loc.gov/2021937085
ISBN: 9780991378012 (hardcover)

Designed by Eleanor Safe and Joseph Floresca
Printed by Bookmobile, Minneapolis, MN
Distributed by Small Press Distribution

123456789

Unbound Edition Press
1270 Caroline Street, Suite D120
Box 448
Atlanta, GA 30307

PERMANENT

for Sasha —

my sous chef, co-pilot, coffee taster-in-chief,
the foxglove to my indigo

Contents

II. Hyacinthum

III. Lilium

Ecologia

I. Indicum

Compass Rose

The wind rose, taking me with it.   Lead in the water main,
two-week old lavender on the windowsill in the shower,
all blue with missing. I was born facing west. A Valkyrie —
sword in hand, blue fire & blue fury,   high winds and thunderheads —
smothered under a century (and more) of grayest skies.
I was so lovely in that life. Not many were the men who dared love me.
Each of them (they passed) like rain over oceans & yet scarred me, so well
that my wings lost every feather, and I became just like them:
mortal, lost on earth, writing songs about the widened sky.
Button-downs, subways. The thrum of monotony that lulls waking sleep
and wakes the sleeper before morning.
Even there they can't stop the heartbeat rattle of the train,
a reminder that you were alive, flew on cloud pine.
I was born facing north, a witch and snow goose, dressed thinly
     because the cold
was my cover: queen over my sisters, speaker to the living and the dead.
Not many were the men who dared.   And the woman who dared,
her red-feathered arrows —   no, you wouldn't understand.
Still I lost every needle of my boughs and fell to earth, studied
to make the same magic from words.
Borrowing them for a time,
they collect under your fingernails like twilight's crystal dust.
You remember, one day, that you came from somewhere else. I was born
facing east. Rode horses & hunted with falcons along the wide plains.
The wind rose through the pale grasses, pressed them back like wild hair.
Arched my back like arrows to the sky before they fall.
And the grace in falling too, as rain comes to rescue.
How many times have I been buried, and come back again?

Stone Fruit

There's no text to be found:
I searched baking shows, science fiction,
dating apps, graffiti on the walls of public restrooms,
literary theory, and didn't carry a word from any of them.
Imagine this: a year in color, but you can only remember black and white.
Or this: your touch is the answer to a prayer,
but each answer demands a new prayer that it continue,
can't be satisfied. Nor can I eat.
Estrogen irritates the walls of my stomach:
I am being hollowed out for a new soul, a second birth,
all that jazz, a woman and a woman who still has to live.

From me comes a knocking sound. And the whistling of wind.

Except I never did live a year in color.
The movement of the waves reckless, sure,
naked on the shore, diving into muddied waters
after a storm.
But that too was a hollowing. A howl.
A storm surge is wordless and when it retreats
it leaves water's signature.
Drunk memories are that way too:
parched mouth, flickering moments,
collecting recollections until they form a flood collage.

Nor did the dating apps succeed. I write *lover* and think
my girl with the wide-eyed stare, who tells jokes in bed,
wanting to feel wanted,
a touch that is the answer
to a question — if anyone needed me —
asked in a letter from my younger self.
The answer, I know, is *no*.
Not that they haven't tried to.

I want to believe the things I say about myself are true,
like *I am a witch, or a queen of spades and tea lights,* I do.
The same way I want to travel to Chicago;
it means nothing until it's in my hand, in my mouth,
not on the page — beyond the page.
Any time I'm whole, I'm also sundered.
Any time I say the voice, the gaze — an unlisted phone number,
shooting arrows over deep ocean.

Nor can I eat. Not explain why I'm halfway underwater.
The note is always different.
Sometimes I quote William McKinley's last words
and sometimes *Fantastic Mr. Fox.* How could anything as satisfied as death
contain me anyway? It doesn't keep down the voices of the dead.
So I hold the space in me like this:
a wind chime ribcage,   a feathered nest for cardinals in snow,
the moment of our embrace. How ginger & how warm.
No, I can't eat. These are my funeral rites.

I am wind whistling through the trees.
A storm surge. It plays in my memory.
Through the ages, trying to warn me of something,
though how could I know?
And when I taste the salt water I taste red wine.
I taste the bitterness of argument.

Let's all take a moment to think what we'd really like to say to our fathers.

Let's all take a moment to exhale.
That is his air. This is his body.
His hollow space, his arms. Name nothing lest it be destroyed.
Do you know what I mean when I talk about the power of names?
It's not grandeur or glamor, but
the mundane, diminished, the dimming light
at the end of day, dying ember smothered
with dish water, a poem mangled by a man's mouth.

So here we are again, you and me.
Howling. Haunted. Laughing. Aghast.
You have love greater than mine for
fluttering. And I have this.
I go through each door, and don't mark the way.
If there ever was a pattern,
I don't want to see it.
Tell me nothing. I may yet change, or be.

In the dark, all mirrors shine crazy and afraid.

Even they don't know who they hold.

Nor see the lack but sense, instead,

the place where the person should be.

That's me: I write about singing and fly

into windows, a dazed sparrow at best.

I talk a big game and then, and then.

I hope you can forgive me all this.

Sleep beckons relief.

It wasn't to be held (accountable) that I started to write,

but to explain what I might feel, to create feeling from

a body of stone, a soured pit, a bitter plum.

There's no text to be found. Any answers still come through the body,

though it barely speaks,

and when it does, I don't know the language of its wild things.

I speak in terms of hurt and heal,

not strings and everlasting, not railway tracks into dark forests,

nor evidence of the moon.

No scientist could prove it.

And you couldn't, either, because it comes down to an echo, a howl,

the cold through spare trees,

the place no one has touched. Not even me:

No, not me, not ever.

Her Name is Red

The time I borrowed from her was wasted in correction.
Edits to those late-night feelings and short stories about meetings
that end in shared showers, falling water, handwritten notes
on the kitchen table. *Stay as long as you want.* But it isn't meant to last
after the end of August, which is to say when life resumes
its course, the stern wind of late summer
insists, one final time, and we all surrender.
I see a mystery in you that's not mine.
First dates outside the café window, trying to find something to hold onto.
This interlude isn't real, less so even than the space between notes,
and pauses in conversation among orchids
in the backyard, where the distance of six feet disappears
into dappled light. And the afternoons swallowed by the ceaseless
creep of autumn. Where are you in that October rain?
And whose umbrellas will I — ? At the dog park and bakery below your place.
I, a cup of black coffee, longing for sun. Your name is red.
Too good to be true.
The undergrads surge back into town, spreading themselves
and their picnic blankets sparsely on lawns.
Only loving some shadow of the oaks, the undersides of leaves
signaling storms each time, the same in each place.
Some things really do repeat, eternal recurrences,
old men dressed in cargo shorts,
with long socks and t-shirts tucked into their belts.
Conversations about faith under trees,
a stillness to the place. Your name is red. Mine, blue.

My Name is Blue

You look younger today, trying to write without capital letters
    (every young man wants to be e. e. cummings
    and every young woman Sylvia Plath):
consider O woman this my body though it has
no answer for you: can I refuse the weapon?
Can the inside of my right knee come unscrewed as I bike
around and around this spatial plane —

thinking, *what pretty leaves   what pretty couples
what lovely titles,*   *is it spring?*   Sadly —
there's no time for that, no time for anything
but murder and creation: my quadriceps and drip coffee,
sex habits, questions posed to the Universe or my Therapist
(look out, the Poet's pissed you're writing about yourself again —
we can verify that No One wants to hear this shit).

You could pick a better place to cry than this,
the wind is howling too loudly the lighter
does not light the center cannot hold etc.
You might remember what you cried for
before the era of   , that it wasn't hormones,
there was something real in you which ached.

This weapon — does your body do *this?*
One weird trick to remove wrinkles
pop pimples   burn fat
get a Bigger Dick a thinner nose
a close shave a scarlet kiss: which means —

you look younger today in that shirt, trying to lift yourself onto your hands
and improve your self-esteem.
Consider O woman that you are what I wish to be, envy —
the misery of form itself does not preclude
its love of someone else. Since I can't do that,
I'll make another body, this one, singing   *time is piling up.*

You're alone in the universe too,
you and History, Culture, Theology
and Netflix's *Too Hot to Handle*. How fine
to pay $6000 a blowjob, we have outdone ourselves
(I would never pay more than $100 for a blowjob).

Not to be reminded of the weapon which after all
keeps quiet in quarantine, except when lilacs, the summer's coming
blooms get me going   (ayyy)
        on sunny days, the gorgeous runners
something about a psalm sure keep talking — I'm listening.

You and I, we aren't so different.
We're the same age,   are cared for by the same Grace.
Pray with me, let *me* kneel, this time
post my content online   flash in public, freedom
from time from the weapon from rhyme from calorie counts,
did I think this philosophy out?

Not at all — it's not meant to live one more moment
or Found a Single School, sweet child;
when I heard the learn'd philosopher
I thought about quitting academia
for the thousandth time.

We played a game ranking our vices
(mom please stay out of this, I get it —
I am not a human until I).
I am not founded madam
by a race of conquistadors, Puritans
and their kinky collars —
        boy did they *fuck* —
now the surface of the thing:
I cut it open ready to dig in,   shining city on the hill,
awakenings, decline, decadence, moralists, hypocrites, part the skin,
nothing.   Shit.

Let me ask you about free will
so I can tell you what I think:
you look younger today without fatalism weighing you down
and a bottle of rosé.
The grackles that live on your porch
are just grackles.

Now, you're alone in the universe —
no Maria Stepanovas, no Walts, not even an Alexanderpushkinbird
perched on some high branch.
Where would you say the singing comes from, then?
A poetic vision? Auditory hallucinations?
Too little sleep? Where, then, the singing, indeed.

My left knee sings an uninjured salutation   (cheeky bastard).
My fingers tremble a little exhaustion.
The weapon is tired and dry:
the weapon has had enough of weaponing,
your items shipped,
your subscription renewed,
you'll forget all about this body soon,
how humiliating to be alive
to shit and think about Aristotle
watch Netflix, play Fortnite —
how humiliating to see the trees radiate green,
knowing something you don't know,
you've never even *seen* a raccoon.

Consider this, madam:
I'll listen
even better than the trees
even better than the wind.

I should have picked a better world than this one
when I was making my world selection.
But it's not the fault of the bicycle
nor is the weapon at fault for its weaponry.
Even the skies are blamelessly blue.
It's not the fault of the bicycle
not the fault of the song,
not the fault of the grackles
(where dwells the breath of all persisting stars
as God comes a loving bedfellow).
It's not a good time for a rhyming word
to bless the sweet green day, I'm permitted to forget everything.

You look tired today,   did you sleep okay?
Did the nightmares keep you awake?
Did you have a new realization about the era of   ?
Did you gather your own flower?

I cried while in a deep stretch:
how blesswretched are we   who live.

Mercy

I'll never be ready, and it's time to start. I don't feel it when the lab tech
draws blood, barely faint, after a few minutes in the waiting room
with *My Name is Red*. The universe isn't going to tell you what to do next.
Nor explain the texts of medieval Rus', your background smile.
Drawn in miniature, the faces of the saints,
shahs, drifting further away from you; falcons, the sphinx.
One side effect is feeling things more deeply.
I can't imagine it – what it will be like,
when I am more than a shadow passing over long grasses
across this world. When you look up, I disappear into sunlight.
Instead the place where sunlight shoots into deep water.
Skin soft as ocean. Feather-light. No, it isn't possible:
I'm already on the brink of vanish and so
will cross that border, sound one bell among the dissonant
chorus of the year of   , the debates and court vacancies of the year of   ,
the vaccines and wildfires.   I'm not a theologian.
I'm not a historian. I'm writing the same poem
through time until something sticks and makes a mark on you:
the number eleven, or the sight of geese coming down to land.
You don't understand it any better than I do.
Believing that tomorrow may still come, and not in smoke or furor.
A hand passes you a glass of water across the screen. I know
we will fail one another, that there will be a reckoning.
A reconciliation. Blessing. Then, as quickly, I don't believe in reckonings.

Each binary, each set of suns

paired for worlds wild as ours. Twinned through time. Born one way,

lost to another. It's easy to perform alchemy. A prescription of estradiol

and church rhetoric. Beyond confession, sacraments, schism and time —

the knife which cuts from one world to the next —

    I want to keep things private.

I rode back with a bandage from the blood test;

didn't pay attention to anything but you.

I could feel my body's future, hair grown out again,

to hold your face in my left hand to see

your clear green eyes. Yes, we'll have to discuss the martyrdoms

    of eastern saints,

the details of their death & worship afterwards. But til then?

Saturnalia

for A.M.

Oh, darling. this carousel city   won't stop spinning.
Nor will we stop celebrating our birthdays —
twentieth, twenty-first, twenty-second, twenty-third —
with bok choy and cabernet sauvignon,
with dumb bitch juice from our dumb bitch flasks,
god bless, goodnight, something about fire escapes and survival.
Would you like to be on my team for beer pong?
I don't think this carousel will ever let us go.
Whatever you do wild and precious in this life,
you'll still be excited about placemats dear,
do you ever really get excited to see me?
Does time stop?   Listen, listen.

It's still going.   The metaphor long since expired
(a blown tire at the bottom of a hill)
but the carousel endures,
from the Long Island suburbs to Century City — I'm a pretty boy
I'm stunning —   we have more forks
the garlic is somewhere in the house   yet the carousel endures
adopts a cat and has its own patch in the community garden,
it dates a future cop and it dates a guy with a young daughter.
It gets engaged and worries about its baby body   tells stories
of grief at the side of the reservoir   (it doesn't jump).

Don't go! Don't take the train
wearing an inverted American flag mask.   Don't go downhill
        as soon as you start, don't grieve without leave. I don't have
        enough time here.
In Somerville, in Spanish Harlem, in Gettysburg then homeward.
                Would you worry, say yes
if I asked you to come with, to live far from home, to stay with me?
I get tired going up the stairs.   I get tired of other people's beauty —
yes, your acne scars and royal nose and bony knees,
thin fingers and love of rope —   I learned so many ties
from basic box to ladder.   I'll stay for a while, maybe longer
if I do. We're coming out, growing up, spending the day in bed.
Healing is brutal, requires a dozen donuts and a bowl to sleep.

She do be inclined toward monogamy. Who am I to say
don't go   when my life is stacked departures,
drawn from the deck in sequence? Train stations are all familiar to me.
Likewise, airports.   I can never get lost, just misdirected.
She do be inclined that way. Works in an ice cream shop,
has that look in her eyes when she chokes you.

I'm glad my wine-soaked self
didn't embarrass you too much.   I'm glad the inexpressible remains so.
in lingerie and afterwards.   Oh, dearest. you know, I think,
how hard it is to feel not only loss.   See flowers dying, remember
this is just one July of all the Julys
I can visit, but not often enough to stop time.
I can pass through eight states in two weeks just to try and get it over with
in the era of   but the era of   will be with us our whole lives:
the yoga and the sleeping in   the evictions and the riots
the protests and the masks   and the lunatics without them
the facetime sex and bike rides   the body writing and rope tutorials
and nobody writes happy poems now   (not about sitting at the reservoir
and talking about trauma   nor about the first time
someone else helped you finish   how much we missed just being held,
have our hair touched,   read and rest my head on your
        shoulder).

The carousel's got pretty lights, pretty painted horses,
and the carousel has the elegance of the Winter Palace, the motion of the sea.
Sometimes I turn, there's only me   and then you shimmer.
This is the last picture (last picture ever).
Yes, I'm still going around. the picture changes: Boston,
the dry and evergreen wash of New England's coast,
New York's mute glimmer transfigured,
annunciations sound into terrible proximity,
roller skating and debating, editing and repurposing,
borrowing and blue. Who can save us from the mob?
Who can recover lost time?   — mornings in bed, a kiss at waking,
one for sleep — I don't need to write a happy poem to describe your taste
at just-so-a-moment; the gate to an expectant sea.
Your hand pulling mine closer to your chest.
That poem would fly away before I could finish it.

Tempest

Like I said, I'm hot wind beneath the stars.
Especially Orion. If you didn't hear or understand
the first time, lay back and drape your legs over the sofa arm,
stretching into her lap while she brushes your hair,
and close your eyes. You know most of it already.
How I hung in sweet air outside a body waiting
like a hot breath on a cold day, except
with time reversed, and the breath waiting, suspended, to enter ...

Maybe shapeshifting is unholy.
If you're here, you might not think so.
I've seen the autumns every year,
how a wet September ruins color,
running them damp and brown into a sigh of a November.
I may have to tell my children
what these autumns, blotted with dust, cold as winter mornings,
meant to us, and what it meant to have this alchemy —
I've been feeling it not in my legs nor chest, but in my dreams
that are, suddenly, runny as eggs, an awful-sweet meringue.

Christ's mother in lament. And not just for him but all the lost children
(of whom I am least). Speechless, in suspension,
flies in amber, an epoch-old bone. Not just a spell or an incantation
but a wave cresting far from shore,
a spray of birds in the same winged cadence, soft as snow in wind,
brilliant light shining on a far-off ocean. An intuition, sure, but also
catching arrows by their sound. Tracking migration by trees' sighs.
Possible, but unlikely.
May your body too never be the same.

So much is possible. I hope you know it.
Even if not now, or tomorrow, it'll come.
I waited so long for this body to hold me tenderly,
and now you, my dear, can be held
in turn. Pierce our feet or wash them, it comes up the same.
The wave, towering, terrifying, suspended in the space
above, where being still was its own pain
& terrible, is now already splayed thunderous
along the beach, and retreats, vanished.
Sudden as hot wind beneath the stars,
or the passing of summer rain.

Austerity

My sexuality is also bicycles.   But mostly birds.
(Especially wet yellow wings). It's pumpernickel bread —
a thunderstorm that finally breaks.
An archive of Franklin Roosevelt's schedules
discovered in an antique shop. A woman-owned tattoo shop,
a tattoo of the nine of swords.   Trusting that you'll text back.
A woman crying under a willow tree.   Alicia Vikander
standing at an intersection — no, not all of her, just her shadow, her turn
as she disappears into the crowd.   My sexuality is how all the women
Wolverine loves end up dying.   A spider bite that won't heal.
A jar of peaches, black raspberry ice cream,
the tear in a cover of a trade paperback,
maybe of *Cyrano de Bergerac*,
and Gerard Depardieu when he says, *'my panache!'* Freshly cut pineapple.

My sexuality is coffee I've paid dearly for. Sitting in a movie theater
with someone, wondering if we'll kiss in the night air.
Haley Lu Richardson and John Cho sitting on the hood of a car smoking,
old *Rolling Stone* magazines,
interesting driftwood,   letting beautiful moments slip away
without a photograph.   Crying during therapy and at family dinners.
Crushing on Irish singer-songwriters via TikTok.   Phone sex where I instruct
in punishment. Bad sunburns.
The sky approaching green after the thunderstorm. Halfway asleep on trains.
Cheap vodka.   Did we sleep?   Do we ever?

Wearing flannels in dive bars.   Getting sloppy in dive bars.
Playing David Bowie on a jukebox and making out with a friend in
        a dive bar.
Neon signs.   Large rhododendrons.

My sexuality is being tired. Crying under a willow tree
(I am the woman).
Long bouts of disgust. Ants.   Ants.   Ants. Ants.
Unfurnished apartments where a terrible crime occurred.
Nobody seeing me smoke.   I don't believe you'll text back,
that you want me to hold you, that any part of me is beautiful.
I don't want to leave a mark on anything.   Walk me to the train station -
ask me to stay another day — so I can say I can't.
My sexuality is not looking back in airports.
Being irresponsible about sunscreen.   Being the only one
in a discount movie theater where *Justice League* is showing.
My sexuality is the summer of 2018,   an inability to let go.
Bicycles left outside an apartment for the whole summer,
gears sticking and switching.

My sexuality is Cate Blanchett in *I'm Not There,*
when she answers questions, looks tired.
My sexuality is missing you   and blue beach glass.
Bradley Cooper in *A Star is Born.*   Being ashamed,
but never shaming you.   All the museums I've never gone into.

The stores I can't afford to shop in. It's knowing you might not come back,
drinking six cups of coffee until I believe anything else.
Ignoring a book so I can watch videos all day, the thought *my body is dying,*

watching Alexandra Ocasio-Cortez answer questions about makeup
and the crisis in Puerto Rico on her Instagram page. Black Calvin Klein
underwear.   Eating with my hands.
Leaving parties early, or not going at all. Walking home on the train tracks.
Not knowing if I've crossed a line.   A cold sore on my lip.
Time and time again making the same mistakes.
Getting frozen.   Not wearing a coat. Of course
I wanted it to be more, to argue about Dick Cheney at the dinner table,
to make things up to each other with red wine   and a granite countertop,
to get tired of one another and give up   then try again
make it hurt   let it go   instead of this.

My sexuality is large brick fireplaces. Buying wine for the price, not the taste.
A way when it doesn't flow. A ship in a bottle.
A ticking clock.   A disappearing regional accent.
Your confusion, right now, as to what this has to do with sex,
because I don't know, either.   A field
cut for lumber where wild blueberries grow.   All the tracks
Bob Dylan left off his albums.
It's Bruce Springsteen singing "Prove It All Night"
and my hair in a long white bow.

Renewing a friendship with someone I went to middle school with,

then letting her convince me to pierce my nose.

It's one hundred years of solitude,

a deep well where a lonely man in his thirties sits

and thinks about jazz.   A book of poems with the same title.

A TV series that hopes to succeed where the movie failed.

Collapsing glass, footnotes, a deep body of referential knowledge.

A legal name change.   Unfortunately, it's Jennifer Aniston.

A failed campaign, a riot, a reactionary government.

Poetry inspired by bad television, the empty place where I should be.

High Holy Days

I still fasted on Yom Kippur the year we broke up.
Swaying in the administrative buildings, on college walk,
resisting coffee's bitter sacraments, trying really hard
not to faint. That year, and the years since, are a novel titled *Folly*
pushing on the edges of convention and calamity,
never going past either.　　　And I still drank coffee
as the sun went down, and streetlights replaced day.
I didn't exist, and still don't,
a candle in a wind tunnel,
in a particle accelerator, in dust & din & ruin, and on the windowsill
when nights are autumn and summer day, like that, a fifty-cent tea light
from Target, blown out.

　　No more need for calls:
they're too sad, even without the international expense, the time difference.
Fuck breakout rooms,
and the moment where being invisible is no longer possible.
Witness the loudest possible person promoted, knighted, and crowned;
they are always wrong about some obvious thing,
like why you'd fast on this of all days.
A novel called *Folly*. And the painted nails are the least of it.
I know alone like nobody,
I know it better than anyone I've slept with, even you.

It's so spectacular. Alone: in my room reading fantasies, visions in color;
walking to and from the library all summer;
the parking lot of the middle school
just before sunset, valley lights;
walking up Broadway and all the way to the Bronx or Jersey.
On trains and buses and subway cars, falling asleep on subway cars,
passing into a Pennsylvania
pocket dimension every late November, eating Burger King at the rest stop
which existed on its own dark planet ...

I'll fast again this year on Yom Kippur. Are you eating? Every meal?
Counting calories, or no?   Still suspended in time?
Believing the world works against you always?
I keep my floors clean and wait days to wash dishes.
Try to keep my silence in any room, breakout or otherwise.
We're not in this world to pretend we are in charge,
to find sadness we don't feel and then write little poems about it.
I like fasting because it takes me closer to you, Lady.
I press my hand against the door.
You can feel my heartbeat. That's not how I know I'm alive,
though: it's you wearing my dad's yellow raincoat,
and reading *A Prayer for Owen Meany* in the library. Challah.
And hitting golf balls in the dark, smoking on the mountainside,
silhouettes spectacular. Trying so hard to be:
the author of a pyramid scheme, political science major,
songwriter, mechanic. I wouldn't change a thing.

The moment of silence after the end has been waiting for you,
with a cup of tea, a sudoku, with an episode of *Harley Quinn*
on HBO and new tattoo ideas, a trip to the grocery store,
your splendid distracted life. Sure, the world comes in.
Ben from middle school and the era of   .

I used to love Fourth of July parades —
like a Norman Rockwell painting —
we all have our heavens. I don't know what mine looks like now:
Dr. Manhattan alone on Mars, or a thief in the night;
migratory birds on the Rio Grande, fires being put out.
An empty highway or the bridge at La Crosse.
The end of a fasting day. Water and bread with honey.
Painted nails and no one to see me;
whether I'm smiling at my own jokes alone,
cooking dinner for myself, cultivating TikTok crushes
that come to nothing.   Fasting honors the space
where people leave you.   When there's still so much
to say, though none of it will matter. All this talk.
These names. Your horoscope for the week says
you're disillusioned, longing for a sacred calling.

II. Hyacinthum

Lockdown

This morning the violets were dangerous,
had no regard for the situation.
Look out on empty streets —
yes, this weather is pleasant. We think this pleasant spring means
more earth —

and the purples of the blood beneath
the skin were dangerous
this morning, lifted high and upright
arching the low back
bending it around the earth like starlight —

the arch of the back was dangerous this morning —
a warm bath
drowning, and breakfast gone cold —
as we disappear, a sliver, an eye, goodbye.

[seven swords and a tower]

What are you studying
in this trying time how are you living
in this trying time
where are you going in this trying time
what have you thought on your windowsill,
and watched the rain to snow sashay

If I could interrupt

The focus here should be on the body
the breath
lengthen the spine   open the chest
dismantle where rib   met focus, craven and intense,
spillage, seep, and nectar —
in the morning after, violets were
dangerous, conversation was dangerous. In case
you didn't know, another person is dangerous —

their lovely cough, and lovely touch.
The corner of the mouth curls into
some cruelty. This is
what you believe. The snow turns to hail,
and another person is dangerous
when met, if they meet, and if the meeting turns to conversation,
and the conversation opens
the machinery, how is it one

and not another is violet, in the sun, wears blue
and o your name so fine
your ass so
fine, in this trying time, a lovely cough,
three spring salmon between us.

        If I interrupt

It was what we intended
and how we did not live, that made the violets
bloom this way.

Speak to the hawk: do you wish
her kills
swift and merciful, and the mice
fat? Whose mercy

and so on —

unlikely, the streets are empty
no deer   no fox   no badger
bluebirds and daffodils

        April is the something something

        Like you said, we were the last generation to grow up —
                it's difficult to explain

the clock tower, the bright flag, the clear air
over New Delhi.

What a time to be alive! What a time to see you only
this way, only one-dimension, as if I myself
were alone in a Midwestern world of half-deserted streets,
muttering retreats of masked foes and friends alike,
the silence that comes and lays across the dorms and restaurants alike
and I dreamed of you on bright screens, the display
picturesque, loving, grotesque,
this is the long sleep, the blue ache, interminable,
and — ? Was that you
sipping to-go coffee, risking your life for a thin cigarette?

        If I could please   interrupt

Say hello when you see them,
my poor New York. My poor New York.
We should have been there, so we could stay inside and watch the fall.

That will be that, that will be the end of it:
Worcestershire sauce and the resurrection — spun webs, last ice of the year,
first in season,
find a position that's comfortable for you,
feel the burn build in your legs.

Just trying to
slow the melanoma:
it's dangerous this year but not as much as
and so are cigarettes

but not as much as   and so is telling a person
you miss them before meeting   but not as much as
and so is a trip to the grocery store   which might lead to
     or a call from your ex   but not as much as
we're on good terms   which might lead to
but not as much as   those dangerous violets.

Lay down
pay me my money down
give me my check
need it to pay for sex   to pay the rent
to feed the cat   to see your tit
what business of it is yours, sir
I did not ask to be born in the time of
and frankly
would have preferred otherwise.

The green beneath the pale breadth of skin
is dangerous: even the flowers arouse us.

[do those mountains look a bit like]

Purity isn't currency,
and I can't buy either
bread nor toilet paper with shame —
were that I was green and red, and violet, and blue,

to paint the nails and wash the face and stretch the leg
change the tire and cook the meat and write the letter
make coffee and drink water and what will
you decide, sober in the time of   .

Someone knows what they want.
It is — a dick in the hand,
a laminated map, a tender caress,
a lasting kiss, a tank of gas, and time to meet the faces
in the places you've not been, to prepare
a face that meets their wants and needs, to meet
in public places just once   never again.

                                        If I could just

A little ride, a little bike ride
along the path,
wasn't that what we planned?

The geese explain it all —
very loud and not into subtlety —
that we have no more time in the time of   ,
no need to stay in touch in the time of   ,
are saying goodbye, goodbye in the time of   .
Saying goodbye,   goodbye —

Ecologia

At this phase in my spiritual development I would like it known
I am not crying   it is raining on my face.
My fathers are many,   all Irish Catholics — almost, it seems, priests
(it runs in the family).   My grandfather often says
he wishes the Pope dead   because he won't let women be priests
(so it runs in the family).
Pops talks about Aristotle and about Plato.
Inside his head — in the empire there.
I know nothing of a man's conscience,
how he reconciles the early days of fatherhood.

I only let myself know this about the future:
        I'll have two daughters
        Katherine and Teresa —
        Kitty and Tess
they'll have to be taught everything,
how to grow vegetables
and hopes, they'll run wild like vines.

Jesus Christ   it's raining hard in here.
        And the Lord said,
'you'll turn me into cherry trees: write this poem   with thy tongue
upon my thigh   *feed thy Lion*   and thy brother   with the Word
which begins   and ends   in leaves of grass.'

I have so many apologies to make   I've made them
I have so many apologies to make   so many laws to break
I have no apologies to make   (I've made them).

Weigh your debt: seventy-thousand for treatment,
a hundred for an education, a million
for the house, and worms in your gut.   Is this how we
were meant to live? Is this any kind of ecology?   Brother
owing brother til his dying day?   "and this soccer field
was a meadow   when I was a boy   why don't we talk
about your mother she was always   a nervous driver
when I knew her   a nervous driver   a bad liar."
It be just facts   *the Word:* thou shalt not slander, nor accuse.

What's true is also so between the lines: there is an ecology
between sound and silence
truth and lies.   In fact, no borderlines at all
just pins and strings on maps   and things we have not reconciled yet.

My wishes into silence were —
for you to see me to know me.
How a line demands to be read,   even in workshops
they do not know how to read poetry   to break a line
to tie a tie
to take a joke   to dream a dream of time gone by
to shake it up baby   to be tangled up in blue.

— were all that I was born the way I ought.   This new life
in which blood flowed   and hair growed
        in sundresses or in jeans
I would still be scarred and burned
and it still would not defeat me
this is my third wish: to be born again facing south,
with miles to go before I sleep.

I bow my head before you Lady.
I have only ever read your Gospels
as a literary text   the Word as lit-ra-cha
like Joyce Carol Oatmeal, dream a little dream of me —

Forty days   and forty nights
and thirst-trap TikToks   (miles to go before I sleep)
before I admit to you our star charts are perfectly compatible.
I am a sucker for Tauruses – my opposite sign –
it is Taurus season, baby, ayyyyy   roller skating and debating,
I got you.   It can rain as long as you want it to
as long as you need rain will fall upon the earth
and become a part of its ecology.   It does not judge.
We shall all be reunited with our English teachers.
We shall all hear from our exes again,
and all those who've ghosted you
will explain that they were just in a really bad place
and it wasn't your fault.
You'll explain the same, to those who you've ghosted.

I refilled my prescription,   I posted that picture at last.
I got some advice about my craft   and ignored it.
To put it another way:
there, at the end, a sign.
What occupies you?   I swear it was an oriole —

Apocrypha

If thou seekest knowledge   get thee to a nunnery, a pharmacy
to buy a cheap bouquet   (on sale after Mother's day).
These are the flowers you need: a rose for romance
a tulip for ancestry. Use an incantation, guided by candlelight.
These are my instructions:
pick dandelions   choose books just to give them away
(covers bent)   and a white bikini   for your man to wear.
Take the hormones that make you nature's true-blue child —

nothing does it now but memory
(comfort and the Word)   nothing gets me there! Nothing!
It used to be that everything & anything
could get a rise out of me, trying a finger inside myself, in the shower,
that's how long I knew who I was meant to be,   how long I knew
I did not belong — to the fist — to the gun —
gaslight, disbelief, the finger in the stairwell.
     Hold me underwater.

I don't belong here: I'll shave my head
my legs   my chest.   Let me show you
humility. My pride undone.   The mechanics of men
working shamelessly.

Don't let the eugenicists fool you.   With their gray calm and natural
selection,
nothing about this is natural,   and nothing permitted of us,
some may never know   the names of their oppressors —
just their counterparts   on TV, great artists and leaders. heroes
        of our time.
Gray calm and devastation: us, part of it, unwillingly
each time I touch your shoulder   each time I wet dream
each time   the shock the skein the fist the tongue
the mouth the eyes the heavy breath the voicemail the mother the father.
(Amen)
I do not know the name of my —   I do not remember when

nor how   it was that some part of me was locked away
and is still locked, still picks flowers in silence   to speak through symbols
to cry each time   someone turns into petals onscreen.
That's how they die in children's movies, not with a knee on the throat
or a bullet in the chest.   No, a cloud of airborne peach blossoms
and release always-a-sigh.   This part of me   wants to be free
to die that way, and soon,   it cannot be undone,
it cannot be undone.   There's none of us unscathed.

A secret under the surface of the skin.
(a pair of ragged claws
on the floors of silent seas).

Terrible knowledge   like, winning lottery numbers
but the opposite of that   if instead of money they give you
cockroaches   and uncles with unsettling eyes
grandfathers who left the seminary
men who came and went   a stairwell   a party
a suspicious glass   an innocuous glass and now
you wish you had been suspicious
a doctor   a dentist   a teacher.

Somebody said   "there's gotta be a *'yet'"*   some resolution
ambiguity that lets us onward some answer
that comforts us
but this movie only lasts two hours
the book three hundred pages, the song four or five minutes
if we're lucky   (and we're often not).

It's all about the Power   until it isn't.
The way the Power weaves into our skin,
makes us gluttons and / or anorexic until it doesn't.
Lives in us and wears our names
until we claim them. Unless we don't   and the Power goes on
growing, and it spreads, in classrooms and in bars   it spreads
      telling you a rose means romance   and marigolds abundance
a heron means your mother is somewhere safe, when you know she isn't,
when a cigarette means   your grandmother is watching Golf in Heaven
when you know she isn't,   when you see that your Father

learned nothing   from all his suffering
Father's Day is the best time
for a picture of you and Beto O'Rourke (he is *daddy*).

If thou seekest knowledge   get thee to a pharmacy,
take sertraline take lithium
take a breather   a face scrub   some time for yourself
selflessly ask the cashier how they're *doing* in the era of
take a look at the woman in front of you
take the time to objectify her a little take the time to correct yourself
and pretend you didn't just do what you just did   take a break from sugar
until your skin gets right   take your partner's sweater home
       with you
knowing it will only make you think of them for so long
take a break from your relationship   to make your partner suffer.
Take a long time to touch yourself in the living room,
think about what you're doing
and how long ago the sex was that you're remembering
(more than a year). When did you last enjoy a summer?

"there's gotta be a *'yet'* where the eugenicists get their comeuppance
and vanity and greed are punished   libraries are well-funded
nobody is afraid of their uncle intimacy is not abject terror
the body need no shame   the creek never blocked
and there is no Power, or the Power is so small that we can pat it on the head

scratch it between the ears   like a fox tamed briefly
     and let it run
rather than swallowing it whole and letting foam come out of our nostrils
and other orifices as it screams inside us   like an alien
popping out of John Hurt's chest   doing a little tap dance
     routine"
(did I get that right?)   I'd like to express what I've been thinking
which is: you think you know   which party I belong to?
Which church which cult which conglomerate?   Tell me now:

     how you can't help telling me what you're reading about
even in the morning, at your worst   pretending you don't want to
needing to walk on my right side   taking ten minutes to decide
on the coffee you always get,   how happiness seems to surprise you when
     it comes,
you never let your phone distract you from other people
     stories mean the world to you even when they let you down.
You always ask and never judge,
never throw yourself off a cliff without looking first,
get deep sad on your playlists until the Italian opera starts
and you google the lyrics to sing in a language you don't speak.

Tell me how to take a deep breath,
I will never carry my own children,
how many children come from the ocean,   how many are born blind.

Yet —

if thou seekest knowledge   I will lay with you in the sun until
we both burn   swim with you in the river til we both drown,
walk with you through town until our feet bleed,   fly with you
     toward home
until we remember where we came from.   Dance with you until
     we are tired
and no longer ashamed   cry with you until grief grows fields of wheat,
endless.   If thou seekest   (if you're looking hard enough)
it'll be clear: close your eyes   the Power can never find us here.

Alligator

Tell me, do you also read movie reviews   after you see the movie
to find out what you think?   Do you wait for a doctor's diagnosis
to tell you what's killing you?
Once it's named, and your mind is set on dying
          (on liking Alfonso Cuaron's *Gravity*) does that settle things?
Or do you seethe quietly,   stand up in restaurants
and walk out on dates?   Does the man who performed perfection for you
no longer come when you call?   You know why:
elegant, selfish, lightning-struck, and cruel,   he's caught midway
biking to the same spot every evening   to read a different book,
he's sleeping around,   he's reading about ethical nonmonogamy,
he's on the dating apps,   he's in partnerships.
He's writing poems of *incredible genius*   thinking about his audience
all wearing fashionable masks talking amongst themselves —
the subculture of poetry, a minor religion   for Soft Dave and
    his acolytes
drawing pencil sketches of the salon.   Oh, darling, *my dirty girl*.

all this wine is for him,   his intrigue and catastrophe,
the stunning realization as he watches porn that   he'S nOt eMotioNaLly
iNvesTed in tHe stoRy   (glory glory hallelujah).
Don't worry, he still finished!   An out of body experience
where he sits and listens to the sirens, and they remind him
of New York,   is still an experience
the love of a Pakistani exchange student   and his marriage proposals
are still an experience,   weeping over his daughter by the sea.

Tell me, do his parents' voices interject as he writes?
His father telling him "you're arranging words in a nice way!"
which is   indeed   what he is literally doing
and his mother telling him "I got stuck on the part about the porn!"
which is   just as he predicted.
He hopes his daughter never hears his voice   or that, at best
it calms her during storms,   or points out birds
or lets her know someone else has made coffee, already,
and it'll be waiting when she wakes,   or maybe that it will tell her
she can fly cheaper   if she takes everything she needs in her backpack.

Tell me, how can he explain all this to her?   Not even the world
with its blood and tears and money —   just the short, painful history
of her own origins.   Maybe he could replace it
with oranges on New Year's and Soviet songs
(lie and lie and lie)   until she dreams in milk and honey.

The sorrow roars like an express train,   this train comes only in
        total darkness.
Rage glows like a phoenix, and never dies.
Your revulsion at yourself sits in your eyes   and makes the world seem
disappointing, because you're in it.   How could your daughter
        ever love
the woman who gave away her womb?   Who muttered the names
of those people and beat a dead tree?   Oh surely she must
        understand
the fury has no bottom,   doesn't give explanations
or make excuses?

Don't you dare forgive the child
in you: *punish her.* punish her for laughing at his French accent.
Punish her for dreaming about raising a family.
Punish her for being disappointed in her own expectations.
Punish her for chasing him around a table.
Punish her for failing to control herself.
Punish her for not being strong enough.
Punish her for being stronger than you are now.
Punish her for needing comfort.
Children need to be punished,   to be destroyed,
                    to weep for themselves by the sea.

Honey, you really don't understand what a body needs
(not someone to wake it up at four in the morning,
to be borrowed and put back to sleep   no ma'am)
and yet you said it was what he deserved   as if he'd died
a glorious death in battle, and won himself a Viking heaven
          filled with maids and maidenhead.
Sweetie   he is a broken toy,
made for nothing   the patient
of many doctors the most patient   of us all,
he has been waiting   these years   to be remade
in the Mother's image and: he may pass the time one way
and you another   but you were made the same,
so, never touch   except to say "farewell,"
          weeping over your daughter by the sea.

Tell me, do you have more words for the song?
Another six months to live? A five-year plan?   Bite down
and cough up   spit up and choke   sit
and write poems of *incredible genius:*   this place isn't home
he has not been there yet   receding into   splinters
the sink is not a place   to store your dishes   we all live here.

Tell me, do you need to get up   every time you sit down?
Waiting for a call from the lawyer?   Waiting for a text from your ex?
What leaves you so restless?   —
Weeping for your daughter in the international foods aisle,
weeping for her in your garden among strawberries,
weeping for her when you finally get to those poems Mike sent you,
weeping for her when your mom comes to pick you up,
weeping for your daughter while reading *Do Not Say We Have Nothing*
    at the dam
            a heron flies at the same time, two nights in a row
            a fish leaps, though only you see it.
Weeping for your daughter ALL THE DAMN TIME,
weeping for her and totally jamming to the Allman Brothers,
weeping for her, weeping for her while scoping out a good smoke spot,
absolutely sobbing while you fall asleep on a mattress with no sheet,
crying your eyes out while shopping for Raisin Bran
and most of all weeping for your daughter by the sea.

This is not a real poem　　　　it came from you as much as he,
it came from the sea　　　　with enough sharp edges to justify
throwing it back,　　　　but it needs to live
to weep to seethe,　　　　to realize it was hurt,
refuse to name its own suffering.
This is where you come from, babe:　　operated on and touched up.
This is where they lie:　　on the riverbank, quiet in the sun
somebody somewhere is trying to understand
how one of those things led to the other,
where they go from here.
They too are weeping for their daughter by the sea.

Tell me, if it didn't matter what you believed,
what would you live for?
He recedes like a tired tide.　　　　Even the book,
the mug, the gym bag, are too much.　　　　He can only
find the energy to weep for his sea by the daughter
see his daughter weep by the sea,　　　　close the door
on weeping as human voices wake us,　　　to make us drown.

Revelation

It's been two days. No, wait — a hundred and fifty-four.
And at the start who would have guessed
we'd be playing drinking games alone
watching the Democratic National Convention?
We have a responsibility to take shots, though no one's watching.
And furthermore, a solemn responsibility to live-tweet.
Oh, go to sleep, go to breakfast,
call me in the morning. We'll find another way to get together.
And even the era of   couldn't make it worse for us,
when we live wherever there are jobs
wherever there is health insurance wherever they will take us
and suffer in these Midwestern cities.
Is that ache in your neck, the cough haunting you for months,
is that a sign of   ? Or just your creeping paranoia.
A flushed fear in the joints that comes at the sight of crowded
        restaurants & bars:
dates that spill into backyards, the growing crowd at frats,
and fairy lights like funerals.
Oh, and the era of   is just a metaphor.

My high-waisted shorts and denim skirt are still in the mail.
Listening to the Convention
one cider in: these platitudes start to sound
like a random word generator fed campaign speeches.
America's eyes have been opened.

I said — *when you disappear* — and I was right, wasn't I? It's been two days.
Scientists and public health officials and contact tracers can't keep track
of those who disappear with you.
In these Midwestern cities of bravado and karaoke bars
and Italian restaurants, these unpublished drafts of chapbooks
never to see the light of day.
Burying my sadness in Taylor Swift and Fiona Apple like the rest of you.
Buying new clothes that I can't afford, like the rest of you,
thinking about adopting a cat.

All the facetime calls seem to end up sad these days.
The cameras take too long to cut away.
The era of   isn't just a bad joke; it's a lot of bad jokes.
It's a lot of governors wondering
whether they'll be able to run for president in 2024.
It's a lot of talk of heroes and lost insurance,
unemployment over our dead bodies,   clogged sinks.
And an entire nation rising like a fever,
running to a hundred and three, out on the street,
in housing court, kneeling in defiance, cut overtime, waiting for the mail,
going nowhere, on fire,
simmering under every masked boozy brunch is fury
from the waiters, fury at gray-haired partisans in the halls of government,
fury. Like the sound of cicadas. Maybe another cider.

And bottomless sleep. The promise of morning coffee.
Breakfast under the thousand trees
of this Midwestern city. When you pray, move your feet.
Here we are on a Monday night. In our great collective living room
thinking we need to collectively vacuum but not collectively knowing when
we'll have the energy.

You almost made it. I-90 instead of I-94. But the fates were against it.
Storms through Wisconsin and through Iowa.
Tornado Warning and you know what's coming.
Time to disappear. Another thing the Convention is like:
watching the audition tapes of bad actors. The best politicians
are actors portraying their love and suffering,
quoting themselves and crossing rivers, if only metaphorically.
It gets tiring to watch. Maybe switch to reality TV?
What are you willing to do to make it through?
Some look more tired every time they come on camera,
as if they hadn't slept in two years. I don't know how to sleep
or to portray my love and suffering to you.
To wear the most convincing version of it
over my skin and fury. Oh, I am tired. Both of dying and of being born.
The sound of cicadas. It's been a hundred and fifty-four days,
four years, a century and more.
And still we can't sleep.

When I do, I dream of shaved legs, aching necks, and murder.
The unthinkable has become normal. Maybe this is the way to show
how much I love you. If I disappear in turn. One day don't come to breakfast,
let the blinds on my apartment stay closed, play drinking games
and run out of cider. Yes, I'll get the skirt,
and shave my legs, and go full ice-queen with my makeup.
My American Dream is one where I die in these clothes,
borne momentarily anew on the lips of politicians
who stare, smiling, into the camera
before disappearing into darkness in their turn.

Voicemail

No one asked me to do this.
No woman shuddering in the cold of the bread line,
no someone on the way to the ballot box —
it's a brisk bright day in early autumn
and, for an hour, time for Old Russian Literature
over Zoom at the coffee shop on Liberty, which was, last year,
just your place. No one asked me to say the way you listen
to someone you find beautiful is also beautiful,
makes them beautiful, like a street lined with one kind of tree
so the colors and light align, and the world seems perfect.
When it's dark I long for a world of voiceless glass,
as all my dreams stay silent, and that must be perfection.
He found another number to call me from.
To make me bend and stretch beneath the face mask,
keeping the most steady I can be. Someone,
brush my hair. Someone, warm my cider.
I cannot speak in any way that counts.
Like in my dreams, I do not have a voice.

And sometimes, it seems, that I was never here at all,
and have been playing some sad instrument
on a chair suspended nowhere,
listening to the strains of made-up music come thinly back
waiting for a harmony and counterpart.
Under the mask I am fluttering. Panic, a tenuous beauty,
broken dragonflies, quick rainstorms, missed chances.
Last night I thought of statues silenced.
                    Should I thank him,
then, after all, for the way my voice
has found its way above water?
The place you can never lose the fear of flood.
Keeps me running, keeps the tightness in the chest,
wary eye: this, the holy ground, the wounded place.

Wintering

Let me tell you what my problem is.
I'm just a woman trying to make my way in the universe,
one who's been in far too many poetry workshops
not to write at least something about her father.
Something with references to Greek mythology —
a retold story where Theseus doesn't leave Ariadne.
And then I'd shake my fist,
or better yet, since I already write birds into every line,
shake my feathers and crow for freedom. I'd write short lines
that break across stanzas, eight or ten in all, each ending on a shorter
and yet profounder note.   (I posted a new picture on my OnlyFans).

She looks at me; I'm disgrace. No amount of scones I bake
in the era of   can make up for a spineless lover,
testing out winter poems on her mother.
You know about snow. But you don't know, I guess,
how snow connects to my freedom or my sex life —
how I flash a quick picture
of me in my bra in the office, while the masked campus outside hovers
under the stillness (like death) of finals week.
I'd pay a fair amount to be told how I'd be fucked,
and a bit more to see it. Forget being bitten!
Kissed, cuffed, grabbed by the collar.   I need it rough.
I *am* asking for it.   I'll gladly plead, tell you a story
of how strong Theseus was, how brave.

Dispossess me of any notions of myth or grandeur —
I've had those conversations with my father,
and he has no shackles, just gray skin
the bleach of chlorine, a trip to the beach for fun,
powdered ashes. So it isn't grand to be free. It's terrible.
Crow? Sing? I'd rather not sing if you're speaking.
I hadn't thought of how much it would hurt to grow wings.
Let me tell you what my problem is: all daddy issues
and no allure. Like egirl magnetism, like Tumblr's heyday.
Living in a moment that's not eternal
a lighted window in an office on a Tuesday night in December,
waiting for estrogen to make me make sense,
or a poem to punch a hole through the window and let the air rush in.
Guess I'll punch a hole in the window to let the air rush in.
Saxophone music on the wintering. Classy friends,
tomorrow's promise of alcohol and submitting papers at long last.

She looks at me, and I'm a lonely acrobat
who can't swing and can't fall.
Help me down or buy a ticket.
Make it a spectacle, since I can't;
I'm just a woman on the floor of her apartment
not woman enough for kissing.
Red berries, cardinals, nimble teeth and slender men.
I draw stares but not enough to.   Cut a figure
though if not.   She kissed a girl (like me).

Static on the record player (no bonus tracks).
I could tell a story about how we are the daughters
of the witches you didn't, etc.
maybe though that the sun and her flowers
spoke
thus
and this
was womanhood, not meme. O thou
shalt be memed unto death. Uptight
without three fingers and spit.
There, your cute slut is ready for you.
Dumb toy, crossed eyes, saint of.

Crying on the floor of the kitchen.
It isn't because I'm Ariadne. You don't
understand. I can't even remember to water
flowers. And of course I cry about the cat
I couldn't keep more than a week.
Things are better now than they were then.
Spoiled eggs   blush and lip gloss,
a drawers of sex toys,   tip-toes,
don't tie me upside down. All the blood will.
On second thought.
Don't cc me on this, I've heard enough from you.
Let the semester end so nothing will change,
I'll coerce a poem from chaos. It'll be bloody,

it'll be romantic, touch your heart, stop your heart,
run a finger from your ear to your collarbone,
even when they die their bones can be reincarnated,
to paraphrase, the trans-lyric is another form being led around
on a leash like a good girl, a good girl, a good girl.
I've been wintering and this is what I wake to!

It's goddamn beautiful.
It made me come so hard.
And even though it didn't,
that reads so much better.
Erotica, not the register, just the melody –
the harmony's part comes from you,
your song, your ecology, not mine.
This is why a poem dies:

it's your wetness, your teenage lust in a closed café,
your garage, your energy, your impulses,
flash, sexy texts,
I've just borrowed you mine a while.
Til cease all motors and the drive.
Yikes.   Like saints.
The heroes have their stories. Each in their place.
This is not for them, though we'll leave a little room.
If they learn how to kneel,
kiss with tongue, my saintly mouth, if they learn what it's like.

But only once they do.

Til then keep them out in the cold, breath ragged in the air

with want, peering through the cracks in the blinds

as we dance in the kitchen.

Lockdown II

This side of lockdown seems much worse to me.
Take us back to those first days of closed libraries,
silent streets, toilet paper shortages,   six hours a day
of video game walkthroughs on YouTube.
Back when it mattered to me who I was in love with,
who I flirted with on Tinder in the Detroit suburbs
before she changed her mind. Now from July, an unsteady unwinding,
as into a ravine.   Yes, into sex, of course.
You know me well enough!   And planned road trips
that don't come to fruition, not for lack
of trying. We should have gone to Chicago over spring break,
should have left this city months ago and wandered the Midwestern states
while they were all still silent and afraid.

Now it's simpler — as if it were still April in our mouths —
and back to the same frightening stage plays on the streets;
we may present ourselves on dating apps more gracefully and with
        the lightness
of sunflowers, but are we light?
Who can we speak to about a long break from either, from
lockdown-just-barely where we can sit in coffee shops
and from lockdown-for-real where snow is our only company?
I can go to the movie theaters again, masked,
and sit in the shadows of rebirth just for those minutes —
the last time was *Emma.* back in March, where I barely watched it
thanks to my momentary fling distracting me — and then, in August,
        she came back

for a while and ruined three perfectly sexless weeks,
then maybe years afterward, while I remember
she *would have* called me Sophia,
had I asked, had she not been in love with someone else.

I still don't know. Besides that: just poems about wet wings and bicycles,
watching from afar, being changed and changing names,
trying and failing to change your front tire, speaking to voters today about -
        being hung up on, starting habits and failing to follow through,
baking carrot cakes, loving you consistently, loving myself
less consistently,   sleeping heavily,
returning to the dreamscape of Long Island's North Shore,
dredged from the bottom of canals,
harvested like horseshoe crabs' blood, sunflowers
that only last a week, light in my mouth like a candle
at the other end of a long hallway,   reevaluating my love
        of Star Wars.
Was it all that time ago I let myself be overgrown
and cared nothing, barely lived in my body at all?

Now it's mine, and this shuddering touch is mine — for me —
for the first time I make myself shake and barely breathe.
It could be - or it could be that my blood pressure is low enough
for me to speak to Her again, slow and powerless.
Didn't you say, powerless — ?
Like it was a saving grace.

Like it was music at a dive bar, and you were trying not to cry
because the lead singer was mostly just a dream you had,
and I was crying because I dreamed
a woman I've never met loved me for a year and a day,
a field of yellow wheat and a poem about tractors.

When you've finished recording, this word
will be the end of it. No more disgraces, in public
or in private, humiliating attempts to bend and break.
I don't think I really understand how it's all connected —
no, it's held, just *there* like a constellation
or a soap bubble.

I think about crossing the border.
Only it would be easier if it were some other far country
to which I might run, and without forms to fill out
and roles to be played I might have already fled — since those
are what I'm fleeing. I don't mind life without sparrows.
Please, Lady, one more kiss that I feel for, fear's hot shower,
elation's late arrival. Sure it'll be that same steady decline into the ravine.
I remember that once a day, just after letting it
get the better of me; now, if that someone
was in the shower as I daydreamed lesson plans
for the week's Russian class, would it have — ?
Of course we dear, know better.

And I don't think we'll ever get to go to that dinner
I keep promising. Not because you wouldn't want to
or because I've finally spent myself out.
No, it's something quieter than that.
It lays curled up under bright leaves half asleep.
It shines down just after sunset
through the remaining greenery.
That's how simple it is.
No, it doesn't matter.

There's no one left to tie my wrists.
You'd be so clumsy if you tried,
I'd probably lose the thread laughing.
You threatened to call me sunflower or baby cakes
but never followed through. So, I'll be turning and diving
like a cloud of starlings over I-94 at dusk barely
visible in the purple evening.
Sure I have the ties under my mattress
but who for? I don't want anyone in my bed but,
don't want any season to end.

This winter under our deep cloud,
no clubs for solace and dancing just loud enough
to irritate our neighbors on the lower floors —
that's why I live in the basement.
Just enough blue sky comes in that I can live.
With instruments and a small library,
with directionless passion, with throw blankets wrapped around me
until I remember that this is my apartment,
and I can turn the heat on whenever I choose.
I don't think I've ever asked myself what makes me fall in love —
more than anything eyes that are also looking
furiously for a way to either love this world or leave it,
for something to set fire to, a way to live again.

III. Lilium

Theosis

I had a conversation with God while shaving my legs
for the first time.   She said, "I'm here to choose your name."
All this time I believed
the search for quietude should end with an emptying.
A renunciation of the will. All this time what I thought
was pussy might just have been the smell of shaving cream.

I want to be a real girl. I want this one thing,
this gift, aren't you a miracle-worker?   I'll give up
anything.   Never write a poem again (that's all I have).
I'll disappear.   "haven't you been listening?"
I don't hear me, I just hear them: my mom asking what I was wearing
my therapist saying you cannot possess anyone
and my dad transforms into a mob of angry men
or forgets my name or whatever   and their eyes are just the same
all their eyes inhuman, the way you look at a murderer.   I guess I am one.

I like shouting into the ocean better.
If this stops at just one page,
disown me. It'll never be read. I'll never be red.
Because even if, right now, I died in my bedroom —
        crushed by a cartoon safe as it fell
from the sky,   you know what would happen.

"so, about your name. haven't you been listening?
I've been trying to tell you for so long.
Trying to tell you that you're right, that I'm sorry it turned out this way.
Fuck, there are so many things I can't even control.
You know the weather in the Midwest? You think *I* would do that?
Believe me, if I could give you one, I would.
Nobody belongs to this world but birds and fish and willow trees.
Remember that orchard oriole you saw last week?
The world is his. It belongs to him. ·   Listen,
you can let go.   You don't have to carry this. I've been living
in a basement in Palo Alto for forty years, practicing the saxophone,
and I still can't get it right. I tried training parakeets for a while,
        I tried working
in a diner. I got rejected by the woman I love.
I'm tired too. I've been waiting in the other room.
I've heard you come close so many times.   I read all the letters
        you wrote.
I want you to be a woman too."

        oh Lady I   (light BDSM is the new vanilla
whose cars do we have? Emily's, Aiden's, and   he said he deserved it
        Tina took this one   named after Sophia, the patron saint of wisdom
there was only one world after all   because a camellia can change
I can't talk if you're singing   it's like you cheated on me

I'm Batman   can this be our song?   rising up

be careful of your skin it's like you're on the right track

and I'm in a city without railroads

so why did you stop drinking   if you leave by the 15th

  you're so nice

the last one is blocked by attachment   I call them arm lunges

just sleep with your roommate.)   Oh, Lady I —

"what if I told you this was already paradise?

That you were being rewarded

for a good life in a far worse world   by your life in this one,

  and everything

you are and will be is not by design,   but the reward of freedom?

  And that

also means suffering, denial, deprivation, high gas prices violence.

You wouldn't believe me, would you? Because that would be too cruel."

I think I would be a great cam girl.

I've been calling and calling from the other room

trying to get some answer. And you come now, while I'm in the shower,

shaving my legs.   I'm falling apart here

coming out   as depressed as trans

as queer. As names for things that cannot be named,

like you and I. You keep asking.   I know it now.

Sophia. Lady, have you seen the video with Riley Reid and Lana Rhoades?
Do you know the cute blonde

who does cool math facts on TikTok? She's a good Christian girl.
How do you keep up with this world?

Does anyone look at you as if they love you? As if they really see you there?
Or are you looking for someone to give you permission, too?

If you can't cum for me, write *slut* on your wing.
cross yourself and stick your tongue out.

It's as real a thing as the sky over Karaganda. I don't want anything, Lady,
just to have someone hold my hand until it's over.

I've given up on wanting things. Call me the name I chose,
just once — so I can hear the need in your voice. (Whisper it to me
like you love me). Whisper it like you want to be inside me.

Blue Velvet

for Liv

I hope you never expose me for what I am.
I hope you'll subscribe to my OnlyFans — seems that everyone is doing it
these strange days, or at least my friends with business sense.
Teaching this lesson in cultural context
like a second language or a new Gospel.
I thought about you spanking me,
and I cried for joy. So relief such dissolution —
I dissolved, that's what I mean,   into subspace.
The knowledge is at the tip of your tongue —

a choker and thigh highs,   I know now what my name will be
when I perform this last high dive — after all the others
from father from mother
from lover from friend.   There is no "at last"
just another night on the computer, looking at Reddit threads
while finishing papers in the Era of

        and they don't seem pointless: none of this does, not the body's love
that fills me up. I went seven miles out,   seven miles back
for a bluebird, the new green shoots, sneezes brought by pollen, geese
        and goslings.

One video of me in the living room. I hope you know
what it means to be seen — to dance on a high wire
and ask you   *would you like to watch me fly?*
I don't even know if I can until you look.
You tell me if I'm a bluebird or.

It won't be soon. It might be in a car,
on the side of the road coming back from the airport.
It might be messy. You might be on top. Someone might see us.
It won't be soon.   You can do anything for money,
but that doesn't make it wrong.   You can buy lingerie
a year in advance. I think I've lost all my right to poetry.
Certain professors of mine would cut these lines, strip it to the bone —
as if bodies were just bone — and the paring of the words
made them delicious, the whole fruit — what about the whole fruit?
My calf, the patch shaved on one leg   by my beloveds.

Grandpa (the dead one)   you'd like this part,
you sick son of a bitch.   I'm not what your genes made me
do. I'm not getting arrested in the park, not this time,
I'm pacing on a sad Midwestern street smoking two cigarettes and
      staring at
white blossoms. I wonder if they
could bring me to orgasm.   They say literature is dead,
but what about — sonnets giving head, couplets that sixty-nine,
my face deep in — sublime — we have no waxing parlors in the time of
not you nor I   just beard trimmers and DIY kits.   I need you

all. Reread what we've written so far. If you feel the need to touch
your cheek, imagine a birthmark there.   I'll leave
no mark on you   unless you want me to.   Nothing without
consent. I am ready to fly. Do you give me permission?

persimmons? perseverance?   play?
One name bites this mouth to bloody.   One name
one flame one sacred hall one scraped raw arm,
can you tell I haven't been biking long?
I should just say: *thank you*.   For being seen.

I hope you never expose me as: a humanist, an ecologist, a follower
of Christ. A woman, a sweet-tooth, an exhibitionist.   I hope
some ancient writer in that long-gone century   is furious
and thinks this poem is a small broken jar   doomed to fail
as humans do, unlike the classics   or Elizabeth Bishop.

I haven't been reading much poetry   but I did file my taxes
and imagine the world as I'd wish it to be.

In Maine   when we were gruesomely young and pimpled
with my long "ma'am?" hairdo and my armful of Jodi Piccoult
you humiliated me   by telling me it was for girls
just so you could read it.
It worked and I was somebody's forever child's pose
at the cemetery   no blossoms   no roses
no orgasm   just *ought tos* and Tiger Woods.

By now you have a Juul and hit it with due diligence
this whole thing has been a debacle
from Easter to the fourth of May.

I don't even remember what the debacle was.
Our family is like that, isn't it?

None of us know how to let them lie.

Smoking with Maria on the porch.
She'd make a good nun. It was her first cigarette.

We pass it on,   we call, we call   and I leave no voicemails —
this is why. Once it starts it doesn't stop.
Talk to anyone long enough   and you'll confess that you
knew them for twenty-nine years
that they have taken up permanent residence inside your heart.
You may forgive me, but your sister doesn't.   I dreamed of
      this moment
but you don't remember the confession, just the rag doll
swinging low   how straight you stand up afterwards.
In the era of   we call and call.

That last letter was a bad idea
      and I know it never would have worked   you see me:
selfish and, at times, cruel.
There are ways of asking for anything.
That happy moment   started with the raspberries
·your grandfather   — may he rest —
it was exactly that — a cup of spiky raspberries on a summer day.

It's always the day of the party   but before the party starts.
We both go home to change.
Christmas lights   card games and vodka,
     keep the food coming someone ran out
for another bottle.   Fix up this wound.
Sleep with me   just side
          by side
in a small bed,   sleep badly, as the drunk do,
sleep badly because I miss   your wild-animal nose —

a soft growl   a kitchen counter   it never would have —

     distance   but what if I had —   then we'd be *really* fucked

I'll drink to that   (to distance)   hear, hear —

This Time Next Week

I'd love to see you sleep with someone else —
to have been invited there, in a comfortable seat somewhere in the room,
and have you look to me to make eye contact while in motion,
acknowledge I was there.
That would be how I knew I loved you completely, darling,
because nothing would please me more than your freedom, your hips,
your completeness, bounded and unbounded, undefined —
without limits —

So many birds come by, just in a minute,   it's like rehab,
or some private hospital for the depressed sons and daughters
of bankers and politicians   who need them kept out of sight.
It's a relief to be preoccupied by red-headed woodpeckers
and bluebirds — much better than the rise and falling of a human soul
on dating apps on thunderstorms.

I'd love to have you watch me — to ask shyly one day
in midwinter, twelve days straight of clouds, whether there isn't something
we could be doing differently, whether we could leave
the Slavic Department of the University of   or the city itself
or the state of   or the whole Midwest:
depart on high seas into a strong wind   roll over whitecaps
and have you watch me, split my jeans open and hold myself
coax the weapon to sing its least dangerous song
as a farewell, as an arrival
heralding January's abandon.

Or drive to Austin. To sit those long hours through —
Indiana, a few minutes of Kentucky
(just a shot-glass worth), Arkansas, then Texas, the weather hot and skies
clear blue, to wonder why we've committed to so many things
when we swore we'd be free forever.   Why not go
to fashion school?   or write young adult fiction for Mormons, specifically?
Why do we just drink coffee from Boston or Birmingham and teach Russian
to undergrads under these gray skies when our souls
are mountain flowers & the lightning   & the cold rain, & all the grasses?
I swore we dreamed better than this for ourselves.

Yes it's like rehab   and the cats, lazing about, aren't helping.
The hot weather as in the humidity as in   even my short hair
          curls, gently.
If you'll be around in an hour, if you don't mind taking the train,
all I have is time and patience, the money in my savings account
and stylish shirts that are wasted in this deep-red county.

We're mid poem, mid leap   midway through
and it's possible to imagine all *kinds* of futures from here
to twist our body   corkscrew pose.
I've been writing haikus   also little corkscrews,
the orchid emoji   is severely underused.
I'd love to see someone else come in   to lie between us
warm and breathing softly as they sleep.

I admit it, I imagined raising children with you
in a suburb of Chicago or New York.
Give me ten minutes in sunshine to let the dream grow wild.

We can't stop until it's done,
and these hard-won barbeques and peaceful fireflies
are no longer laced with terror,
until I no longer need to slip away from family gatherings
to smoke a cigarette.

I'd love to be chaste for a year, the way I spent a year getting sober
only to start in again on the rosé,
just to understand some things before I forget them again.
And if we live a week in silence   or even two
it doesn't mean the end of the world:
I will still have stories about birding
and the cat will still bother me at my laptop.
I will still get my fancy coffee and try to make you remember
what it was you loved about this country.
I will tell you that you are not chaos, not cruel, not darkness incarnate
and you will, as always, not believe me

I don't know if you know how long I waited to be touched
and how afraid it still makes me,
I don't know if you realize how little power we have
though you know he isn't smart, but beautiful   poor baby,
how could someone grow up so kind?
Why would he drive me home afterwards?

Sometimes in darkness, sometimes in light.

Give me a ride   I'll sweep you up in my arms
we'll celebrate for a year and a day   under the aurora borealis,
the midnight sun   the midnight sun —

Spolia

after Maria Stepanova

They're all at home, so am I:
I haven't gone out since April I
haven't left the bed.

The borders are closed indefinitely;
we'll stay in Nur-Sultan, in Almaty.
We'll stay until he lets us in
in Tomsk in Murmansk on Sakhalin.

To live on a twelve-hour difference
means to wake idly and in urgency sleep
at the foot of the clock tower
demanding haircuts
"we demand haircuts"   as *if.*

But sure — I'll get you laid, make your bed — you sleep
in it, unfold the auspices of white lice, you parasite.
this lockdown is really
such a blessing in disguise   (people live such different lives).
When your house is drowned, the landlord
raised the rent, so sleep in a tent
or in your mother's basement,
which she doesn't own, either.

From sea to shining
curbside pickup.

The lives we put at risk,
my fellow Americans, don't cancel my golf season
or lick your lips at the sight of the rich!
The borders are closed indefinitely.

This is how we pass the time:
come up with puns,
put out their eyes
turn on a dime – and RIOT.

This is how we pass the time:
Pornhub Premium is free for everyone but Carole Baskin.
she can only Get Off on the free stuff – as *if.*

Just like you and me!
a homebody and nobody
who made good
just like you and me!   (people live so differently)

You don't know the names of your neighbors
you keep quiet in church
you praised the Lord
and played his little games — til now.

We were made in deep snows
we pass the time in deep snows
we made videos of ourselves in deep snows
making love in deep snows
Fisting in Deep Snows
Rimming in Deep Snows
Shibari in Deep Snows.

Quiet now, don't howl.

The lives we put at risk,
one might say they had souls
bigger than the empty space inside you, bagel-like and
slathered in turmoil —
creamy turmoil   with garlic that
unsettles the body unsettles the mind.
Thank you for sharing your practice with us,

Carole Baskin
        (but it isn't *timeless* isn't *true*
        won't pay for that new
        haircut, won't
        ask how — quiet now, don't ask
Carole Baskin

who's killing who here?)
I took my haircut into my own hands
and making love
and all the rest of it,
woo hoo   woo *hoo*.
Skinny dips at the Docks
you know where   you know whose,
are not enthused, silly lovelywet and wild
tenderize me
I
a child
of heaven.

Yet it snows,
it may do so all year,
things are leaning that way.
Just a human voice (people live — they have no choice)
singing in the shadow of blue.
Do you think it'll snow all year? Do you care?
Honey, I'm barely buried, and you've made off with all I had:
three sisters two hounds a cock a downer ending
for the first round of shuttered stores and system time.

Who will take longer to deal me my final Hand
Gamestop or the IRS
Pornhub or FX's *Devs?*
I hung up rather than shoot the messenger.

The Lord dropped his handkerchief
that one might see it and say *sanitize that motherfucker —*
quick!

The Word didn't belong to King James
nor to naked nor to madness
(how do you do yoga? —
I light a single candle, strip, and burn my thighs to bits)
not to Luther nor Erasmus
(how do you make reading lists? —
I follow the spirit, kneel before the shelf)
nor to Baskin! Who dreams of tiger skin cocks
forests and jungles, gin on the rocks, am I
repeating myself — very well, I repeat myself.
I am large, I contain multitudes:
when the lilacs in the dooryard bloom'd
we find another home
where'er we so choose.

Spoiler alert: the end cometh.
It comes in spades and clubs, wands and pentacles.
It deals its hand. It shapes the land. It curses you entirely,
from head to foot. To live bodily. To want.
To be alone inside the shell.
It crushes it, it twists it, it slaps it once
then falls asleep, the beast!

Quiet now,

    quiet now,

        don't howl.

I lift the flower to my eye.

The fury, fire, secrets and psalms.

You don't need to see where we've been

to know what we've done.

You don't need an eye or a tongue

to taste or to speak.

I'll do you one better — breathe in.

Quiet, quiet now. Oh howl.

How ginger, how secret, how warm.

Quiet,

    quiet now,

        howl.

I'll bring you the spoils of war.

Mercy II

I've been thinking about mercy — how hard it is to forgive
Sylvia Plath her death, perched like an owl in a stand of trees,
while below her, soldiers search for fugitives, her children
nestled tightly beneath her wings. I don't remember often how you, too,
almost died that way, how if it had been entirely in your power
the X-acto knives, wisdom tooth surgery, and climate of silence
might have left you too gazing in a full circle, preying on field mice
and hushed under falling snow in some other world. One without
    cities, hurry,
addictions, Catholicism, bread-breaking, me and my faceless miseries —
this is what I think about when I think about mercy. Arrythmias,
temporary blindness.
You're free now, anyway. It'll be warm all winter in LA. You and
    your parents
can bake, play word games, watch season two of *The Mandalorian*,
take your dogs on walks around the block in the browning shadows
    of twilight.

I'm sure you have no mercy for me in letting go.
No forgiveness for the intuition that led me to diners on January nights,
Marriage Story despite your protests, Lumineers concerts.
No mercy on me for my beginning,
today, in fact, when all the promises and poetry come alive like miniatures
on the page, martyrs, priests, gold coins and yew,
elm, birch, pagan lights, fires through distant trees, drums and rage,
my wilding, my resurrection.
I pray the same sometimes:
I know the same eternity sleeps inside you
like a line of long-dead kings and their fathers
stretching back to some Charlemagne. It moves further and further away —
the mirage of water on a highway — the hope of mercy for ourselves,
tender partings, rather than drifting through time.

Go with the Lady, and lovely onward. I don't need your mercy.

Ecclesiastes

We are in a state of the sublime,
watch the snow raise itself up, then stretch itself in nets and webs.
How often I lay on the floor and the streams wash away —
How often I lay on the floor and the rain washes away —
How often I lay on the floor and your daughter, sir, washes away —

If I told you Lady I was in a state of the sublime,
a standing split in the Era of   *the Lord, my boy, doesn't make mistakes*
                        or female priests
and realized your mistake   *or gays or queers or tyrannies*
then what about me?

And wasn't Emily Dickinson a blue priestess
who spoke to the little wide-eye gods
that live in oaks, aren't her drowned children
in every stream, and in agony on the webcam? Sweet summer
child: the Lady doesn't make mistakes.

We are in a state of the sublime:
in ecology, in time,
no written word suffices.
You're the father of this crisis,
blue priestliness, a poem, a sink, and soap
to wash the first shame of body away —
your daughter, sir, has a dead name,
and twenty-three years in your mouth.   *Would it not be easier*
Touching blue death and sparrows.   *and I ask you would it not be easier*
A bird in the hand does not.   *to shave your head*
A bird in the bush does not.   *join the club?*

How rugged the woman that strides these hills
stripped of agonies and terror.
She, (unlike her mother) she
will enter the world, leave blue traces and blue notes.

The snow does not come steady down,
nor spring in sure progression —
distance brings a body down,
a priestess bearing children
in the womb of poetry.

Yellow Chrysanthemums

I turned on the heat in my apartment for the first time this morning.
I've yet to take a bath here. A bouquet of yellow chrysanthemums
sits, a little fountain of late-September color, on the kitchen island.
I've had to assemble more by hand than usual: a new bookshelf,
that island, a new bicycle to replace the one stolen from outside
the grocery store. Objects become part of you so quickly.
This couch already has a history of sex, of wine, and watching
Luca Gudagnino's new HBO show, in half a season, less than that.
It holds a future. Light declining steadily as the equinox,
then the solstice pass, renewing, snow falling outside on quiet streets,
friends returning from abroad, an election and its horror –
my sister texting me FRAT and a friend with a dilemma, more wine,
no doubt, and that yellow-chrysanthemum love I have for you,
the celebration of abundance as the calendar year passes by, again,
Mars in retrograde, the circumstances of seven-hundred years,
an ocean composed of moments when we do not pass each other by,
but complete full circuits, spiraling upward like rebellious angels through time
toward the places and instants our decisions have led us to —
toward the bars full again on Halloween, toward further rioting and
    riots of color
as autumn comes and we are free, toward a year on fellowship,
full time jobs, changing cities, and then — remember that first apartment?
And movie theaters with waiting-for-a-better-time marquees?

How *Tenet* failed to save Hollywood and slowly we drifted each to our
    own orbits,
Taiwanese new wave cinema, sad girl summer on Spotify,
documentaries about whales, Traverse City cherries,
existential crises about grad school, appearances, doubt,
Doc Martens, yellow chrysanthemums. The sex,
so spectacular and devoid of romance,
so tender and so furious. And the dinners I have cooked for my friends
as they visit me for tarot readings. The same mistakes —
the same mistakes. Yes, remember the stacks of books I waited all winter
    to donate
to the library? The letters we sent to undecided voters
in the hope they still lived
at their old addresses, that our handwriting wouldn't get thrown away
and how we made calls into North Carolina, New Hampshire,
and Maine? A week or two that flowers last. I have no answer for you
    but this love
and the weak-kneed feeling when you call me *babe* during class,
as our professor's hair fades in and out of the green screen, an image
of a church in Kiev, and something about the lives of saints too dull to bear
without your face above, an icon, the patron of lost time.

Foxglove, Indigo

Forgive me — I have no one to write letters to in the spin and silver
on the river's slim surface, nor in dragonflies, not aloft
held by wheeling hawks or buntings hopping through the brush,
nor thrush accomplishing his errands. This will have to do instead,
only & for now replacing the green veins of trees and the song that takes
a decade in the singing. I ride rusty bicycles and walk dusty steps
below these eternities of forests, discarding another season's sheath
like so much tattered clothing. Were I to try and turn these movements,
moments slaughtered still by sunlight, relegated to a willow rather
after blinding me in glory, then I would say —
before you I knew hunger, and since you I knew what for.
Say that until you I had tasted without savoring,
and now the air itself inebriates. I hold stories for you all day.
Lichens write it better than I do, tired holly in the dry.
And yet each burst of poison-red against the winter sky
is an exclamation point on my behalf, to you, you alone.

You'll be the first to tell me there's no such thing as foxglove, indigo.
This betrays you first, arrays your slim hand (a pen there grasped)
in opposition to the futile pout of your always-mouth in waiting.
Bothering with words beneath you.
Who needs a conversation to describe the lilt and tinder
of the cotton-dragon lavender of evening and our final coffee of the day?

Not you, just I
working from the outside in to help the words make something grow,
sowing seeds across a field early in the morning
after daylight savings time —
planting late for a January harvest,
when we start to trade day back for night again.

I *am* blind without these lights illuminating the surfaces of things.
Keen sure on the deep-down way of people —
their secret cities hidden in reflections,
their wild mountain-lightning and the flower
that wrought it —
yet to scavenge one tablespoonful ache of love
forces me to break the shell, to pry, devour, to seethe, to wrench,
to weld, live it all a second time.
Saintly and angelic you are not. Prefer me as I prefer you:
the humility of maple trees, the not-quite forbidden dance.
Oh and all our cigarettes. I blue and yours without looking back.
My foxglove, my indigo; my colorblind, my ocean child.

This is the angel of it all, you are mine already, that your apple-sweet laugh
falls into my hands, far too much to carry, that your shoulder falls
        from below
your loose blouse — these are the words I wish I could write
and that fail, as everything, in meaning.

Whether it was you yourself or just the feeling.
Whether it lived or died.
I've said what's necessary, so dance again as lightly
as speechless as a parade of shooting stars, or leaves
swept up in determined and silent wind.
Let nothing you dismay.   Nor burden it with undue ties
and catechisms: what kind of prophet,
loose-lipped and flirting, would I be if I had any whatsoever answer?

You know, whose I am. I had no one to write letters to yet
they wrote themselves. Especially alone
when I was waiting for this moment —
the soft hand beckoned just for me
to arrive here, to land and not to bow before anything
nor anyone at all. Your pride as fierce as every lion.
Even a power you didn't know:
to blind, to reach back in time,
turn a woman into a willow tree bent both
by sorrow and by laughter, and make foxglove, indigo grow.

Kenosis

She need not speak to me now.   I've shaved my chest for our date
and flecked my hooded brows with gold — as if even that were necessary
for the warmth pooling in my living room to lead to kisses,
to hear my name as it was meant to be said.   And I chose
emptiness that meant something, in place of the hollow noise
when I was called and called and could not reach the surface.
A renunciation of the will, and something in me grew.

          It was: vines, depth, a yearning for your fingers inside me,
anything you wanted, your hands on my neck; what would it be otherwise?

And now I know the smell of pussy, the smell of my whole body,
of my armpit hair and breasts (even the honeysuckle three months from now
will smell of it).   Haven't you been listening?
I didn't live this long to die a suburban peaceful death,
some grim man wondering where the body in his heart had gone,
why his empty hands stayed cold, not listening
to the whispers of his — her — *my* name, my wisdom,
my grief, the oceanside   of tears not yet shed
for all lost and gained.

I've been trying to tell you for so long.
It had to turn out this way.
I had to pray twenty three years under the deepest silence
the world has ever held its breath through and wake,
fully formed, skirts on the high line, purple lingerie
worn inside-out,   and the falcons that come to land

in trees and the wind of a foretold March recognize me now,
even if the company of humankind on the streets doesn't,
even if this may end after a single page, because we can go easy.
We can be gentle and fierce as lionesses in our way.
Trade power for power and no one is prey.

(Because even though it needs to end, it's been beautiful?
we broke down in Montauk, please come get us   high speed rail
        that's my translation, anyway   a light whispering rain
you look absolutely beautiful   coffee suffer sleep
eat write fuck   are our grades up yet?   I prefer living alone)

Lady, I knew all along there was something missing.
I loved it all so dearly (I do), the rush of wind in the trees
on otherwise still nights,   long stretches of highway
winding through the mountains, my waist and curly hair and openness.
It won't be cruel any more.

I've been silent from the other room.
Your hand, bathed in light, is gold.
There is no other world at all.
And no one left to stop the song from growing.

It's been wintered all this time,
in the ground,   buried in deep sorrow,
a dark eternity of sleep
stretching back to some Norwegian king saddened on the throne
by time, whose tears grew women from the ground
(my mothers, my father).

Oh, Sophia ... and much more than that — that your name too is mine
for nights and then released.
I'll be very good for you (it's what I want to do).
And first of all I know I am loved,
and the world must try its best to keep up with me,
to let me know that it has loved me all along.

I will tell you exactly what I need.
Come to me and take it slow — make it last all night
and into morning.
You and I disappeared into evening then — stars
and their forges, iron and another year.
This one, and my old self, are resting now,
silver coins over their eyes. I am the one
left to see them. I loved him well.
May he rest. He sleeps so I can live.

Acknowledgements

First, to Patrick Davis, my publisher at Unbound Edition Press, my eternal gratitude and respect for your patience, love of poetry, and willingness to take a chance on an unknown and very young poet making her way in the world. This book would not exist without your vision and enthusiasm.

To my mother and my sister — you have both been reading my poems, good, bad, and bizarre, since I was sixteen and wrote that first emo ode to rejection. Not only have you believed in me, but you have believed in the poems. This book was born with you watching over it.

To the friends who have become my family over the years — you have been the reason I've laughed all of my laughter, and cried all of my tears. My life belongs to you if it belongs to anyone in this world.

To Yaël in particular, who designed the image for the dedication page and blew my expectations out of the water — I will be submitting my request for another tattoo design from you ASAP!

To those whose words inspired me and who I try my best to honor in these pages — and in no particular order — Walt Whitman, Emily Dickinson, Terrance Hayes, Tracy K. Smith, Sylvia Plath, Bob Dylan, and many more — you have laid a long road, at the end of which I now place a single stone of my own making.

And finally — to my transgender siblings in this life, whether you are out, or just beginning to understand the roots of your own true self in private — you are so extraordinary, so beautiful, so powerful for surviving this far. Honor yourself by accepting whatever help you can get, trust your own intuition above all else, and keep living. Everything else will come.

If you have the financial means to do so, consider donating to these resources for LGBTQ+ people of color, who face the most systemic violence in our country and world and are in most need of aid:

The Okra Project
Solutions Not Punishment Collaborative
For the Gworls
G.L.I.T.S
The Marsha P. Johnson Institute
The Black Trans Travel Fund
The Sylvia Rivera Law Project
The Black Trans Femmes in the Arts Collective
Transgender Law Center
TGI Justice Project
Brave Space Alliance

About the Type and Paper

Designed by Malou Verlomme of the Monotype Studio, Macklin is an elegant, high-contrast typeface. It has been designed purposely for more emotional appeal.

The concept for Macklin began with research on historical material from Britain and Europe dating to the beginning of the 19th century, specifically the work of Vincent Figgins. Verlomme pays respect to Figgins's work with Macklin, but pushes the family to a more contemporary place.

This book is printed on natural Rolland Enviro Book stock. The paper is 100 percent post-consumer sustainable fiber content and is FSC-certified.

Ecologia was designed by Eleanor Safe and Joseph Floresca.

Unbound Edition Press champions honest, original voices.
Committed to the power of writers who explore and illuminate
the contemporary human condition, we publish collections of poetry,
short fiction, and essays. Our publisher and editorial team aim to identify,
develop, and defend authors who create thoughtfully challenging work
which may not find a home with mainstream publishers.
Guided by a mission to respect and elevate emerging, overlooked,
or LGBTQ+ authors, we work to make meaningful contributions to
the literary arts by publishing their work.

unboundedition.com